This book belongs to:

_____

BUTT ARTIST

To Becky for her loving support of me and this adventure.
To Madeline for inspiring me with her art and enthusiasm.
She is Everything Butt Art's biggest fan.

- Brian

To Marilyn, Jay and Anthony for encouraging me through
(i.e., tolerating my) years of manic and disorganized creative
development and to Bob Case for showing me how to tame
the beast into the dream.

- Alexis

What can **you** draw with a **butt?**

Everything!

everything
butt art

at the ZOO

You can bring a
ZOO to life using
your imagination,
some **creativity**
and...

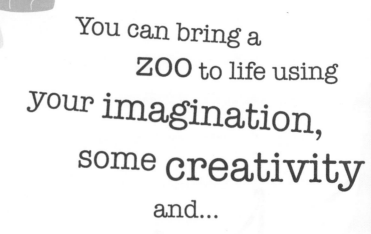

(a but

Always start with a **butt!**

1

2

The pink lines show you what to add in each step.

3

4

5

6

The ZOO
is full of
hidden butts.

See how many you can find in a game of ButtHunt!

MURPHY BUS CO

Field trip to the zoo!

Next time you're sitting in the back of a school bus think about this: a green anaconda, the world's largest snake, would stretch from the front door all the way to your seat, almost thirty feet!

A chameleon's tongue is so quick she can grab her food faster than your eyes can see

1

2

3

4

5

6

You'd better keep a close watch over your ice cream!

Watch out, little bird!

An alligator can propel himself out of the water
with his powerful tail, grabbing an unsuspecting
bird right out of a tree.

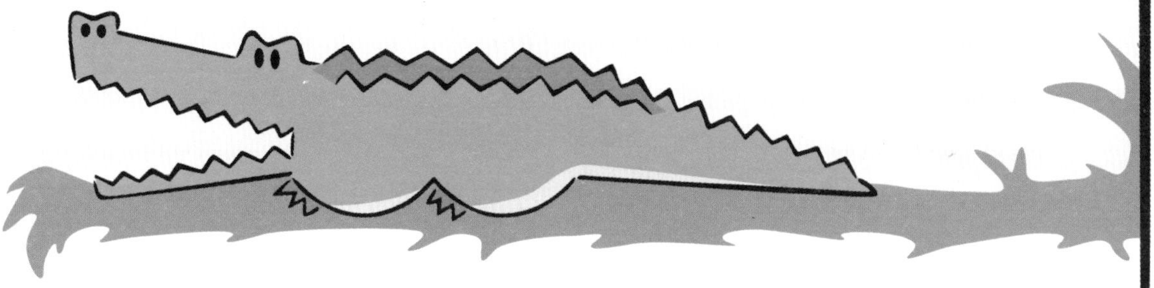

1

2

3

4

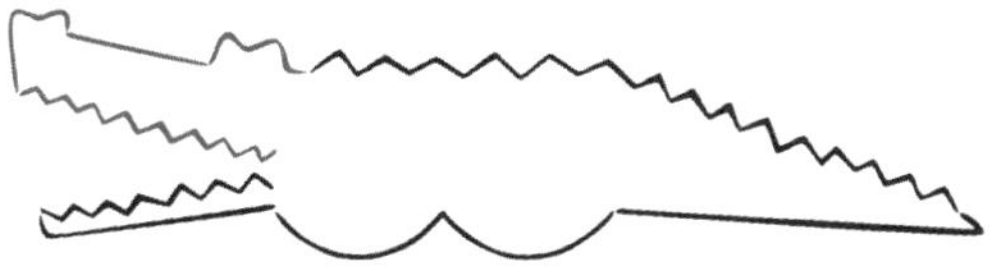

5

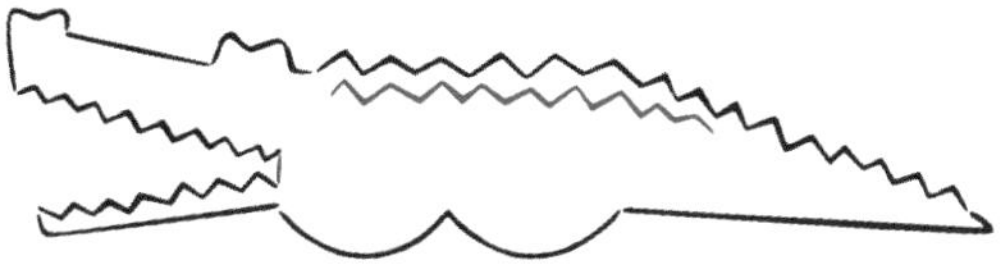

6

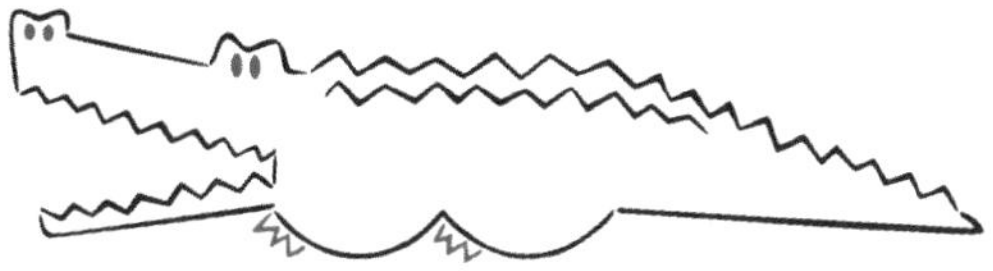

Reptile

Though they may be hard to tell apart, alligators are all unique. Spot the differences in these two alligators:

House

Can you find all the reptile-related words?
They appear sideways, upside-down, downside-up,
backwards, forwards and diagonally, too!

```
G T A N A P S I D S G N U T
C O P P E R H E A D K H E N
O R Y A Y S Q A R B O C X O
L T T O F R I U C G F R R G
D O H P A T C K B D E O D A
B I O J N Y H L O R T C S R
L S N I G U A N A A A U O K D
O E L T S B M E G Z N D I O
O W H U T T E I S I V I N D
D I U R N A L Y C L U L K O
E R A T T L E S N A K E B M
D G I L A M O N S T E R M O
N Z G E V E N O M O U S T K
C O N S T R I C T O R M T
```

chameleon
alligator
crocodile
cobra
rattlesnake
iguana
python
lizard
egg
tortoise
skink
komodo dragon
gila monster
copperhead
fangs
constrictor
venomous
gecko
diurnal
anapsids
cold blooded
turtle

1

2

3

4

5

6

Do you use sunscreen at the beach?

A hippo does too!

However, unlike you (unless you happen to be a hippo), she doesn't buy lotion at a store. Her skin makes its own red-colored sunblock.

A gorilla consumes nearly forty pounds of food daily. Imagine if she ate only bananas. That would be about 160 bananas each day! A gorilla also eats seeds, termites, grubs, and caterpillars.

Do you think a **caterpillar** would taste good?

1

2

3

4

5

6

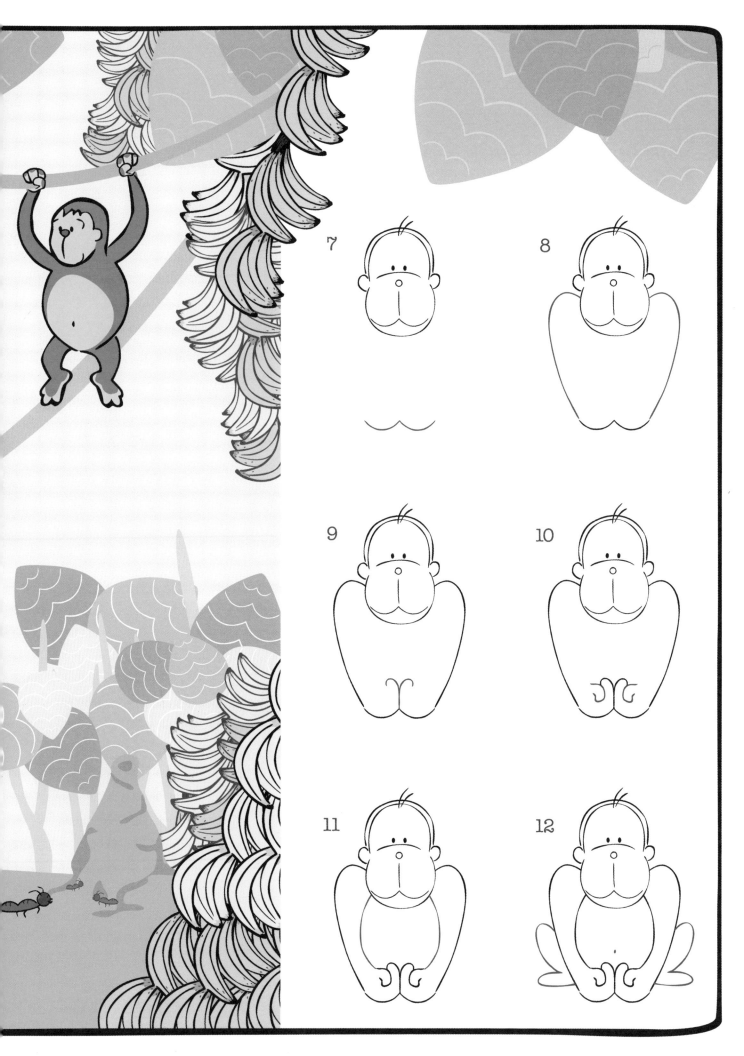

7

8

9

10

11

12

Does hanging out in a hot spring or rolling snowballs down a hill sound like fun to you?

1

2

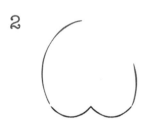

3

4

5

6

It's fun for snow monkeys, too!

What do those silly apes do all day in the

Primate Pavilion

———— — — — — —

Decode the answer using the key below.

a =   b =   c =   d =   e =   f =

g =   h =   i =  j =   k =   l =

m =   n =  o = 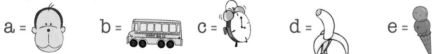 p =   q =   r =

s =   t =   u =   v =   w =   x =

y =   z =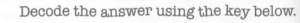

Connect the dots to reveal the baby gorilla's favorite snack!

What a fussy eater!

Ninety-nine percent of a panda's diet is bamboo. With such a low-protein food source, it's remarkab that he's an excellent swimmer and rock climber.

Tigers, the largest members of the cat family, can be as long as eleven feet. Unlike a cuddly housecat, it might not be so cozy to have a tiger sit on your lap.

Wow! That's a big cat!

How high can you jump?

1

2

3

4

5

6

A zookeeper can jump about 15 inches high, right over a tortoise. A kangaroo can jump more than seventy inches high, right over a zookeeper!

Parrots and
toucans and
cockatoos, oh my!

1

2

3

4

5

6

There are thousands of bird varieties in the world. It looks like they're all arriving now.

How colorful!

His powerful legs help him run almost forty-five miles per hour.
That's over the speed limit on many roads. Despite his great land speed,
he'll never get off the ground. The ostrich is completely flightless.

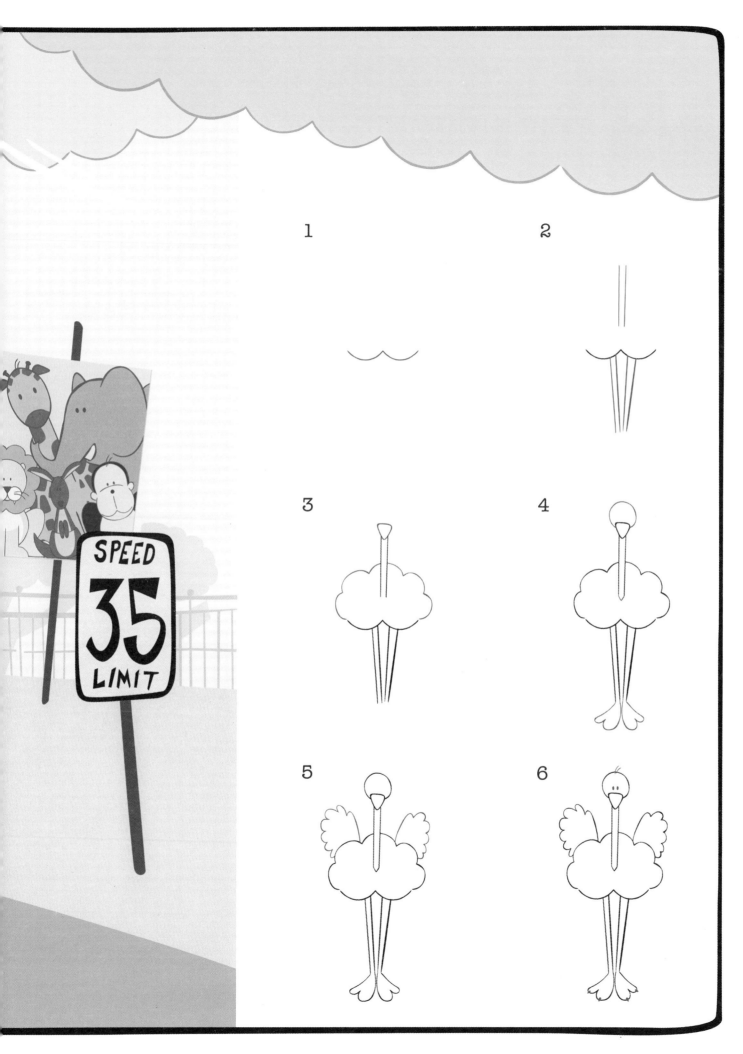

1

2

3

4

5

6

SPEED
35
LIMIT

Aviary

Color this dodo by numbe
with the feather ke

Use the clues below to fill in the bird-themed crossword.

CROSS

bald scavenger
each bird
birds eat with this
often yellow with a beautiful voice
cuddle in pairs
early bird gets it
symbol of peace
red chest and blue eggs
bird's bed made of sticks and stuff
not one can but...
ostrich's Australian cousin
a roost and type of fish
hard to fly without these
green fruit and flightless bird from New Zealand

DOWN

1. large bird enclosure, sometimes called a "flight cage"
2. birds wear these
4. fast running and flightless
5. hawks can, penguins can't
8. pirate's pet
9. pink and balances on one leg
16. whooo, whooo!
18. baby birds hatch out of this
19. home to birds and branches
21. sharp claw
24. keen-eyed bird of prey

Despite having the longest neck of any animal, the giraffe's mouth cannot reach the ground unless he awkwardly spreads his front legs.

Steady big fella!

1

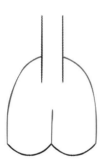

2

3

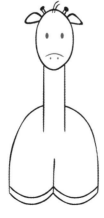

4

5

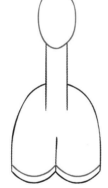

6

Shhhhh!

The lions are asleep at the zoo.

No surprise! They sleep up to twenty hours a day. But, with canine teeth over three inches long, lions can be fierce predators when awake.

1

2

3

4

5

6

At first it doesn't seem so because he hides in tall, green grass. However, lions are colorblind, making a zebra's stripes the perfect camouflage.

Unscramble the names of savanna dwellers below.

TEACHEH _____

AFEFRGI _____

NIRERSORHO _____

BEZRA _____

NOLI ____

TANPHLEE _____

EZLAGLE _____

BLEISWETED _____

NEHAY _____

RGATOWH _____

Help the hungry warthog reach the delicious insects!

Did you know that an adult elephant weighs more than a car? It sure would be funny to see the zoo parking lot full of elephants!

Beep, eep!

1

2

3

4

5

6

answers

Reptile House

Aviary

answers

Primate Pavilion

<u>m</u> <u>o</u> <u>n</u> <u>k</u> <u>e</u> <u>y</u>

<u>a</u> <u>r</u> <u>o</u> <u>u</u> <u>n</u> <u>d</u>

Savanna

TEACHEH <u>cheetah</u>
AFEFRGI <u>giraffe</u>
IRERSORHO <u>rhinoceros</u>
BEZRA <u>zebra</u>
NOLI <u>lion</u>
TANPHLEE <u>elephant</u>
EZLAGLE <u>gazelle</u>
LEISWETED <u>wildebeest</u>
NEHAY <u>hyena</u>
RGATOWH <u>warthog</u>

This book's cover is made from 50% post-consumer recycled paper.

The interior pages are made from 100% FSC certified eucalyptus fibers.

Using recycled paper saved 6 trees and 2,748 gallons of waste water!

(find our full environmental audit online)

Mmmm, eucalyptus!

8,500 copies printed in Rochester, New York by Monroe Litho.

Sharing & Saving

There are so many ways to share your Butt Art drawings with the world!

Here's how:

Go to everythingbuttart.com
or
download our iPad app

Create an account.

Take digital pictures of your art.

Upload images to your private gallery or share them with everyone.

We'll save all your artwork so you can see your progress over time!

You can also email your work to share@everythingbuttart.com

f or post directly on our wall at facebook.com/everythingbuttart

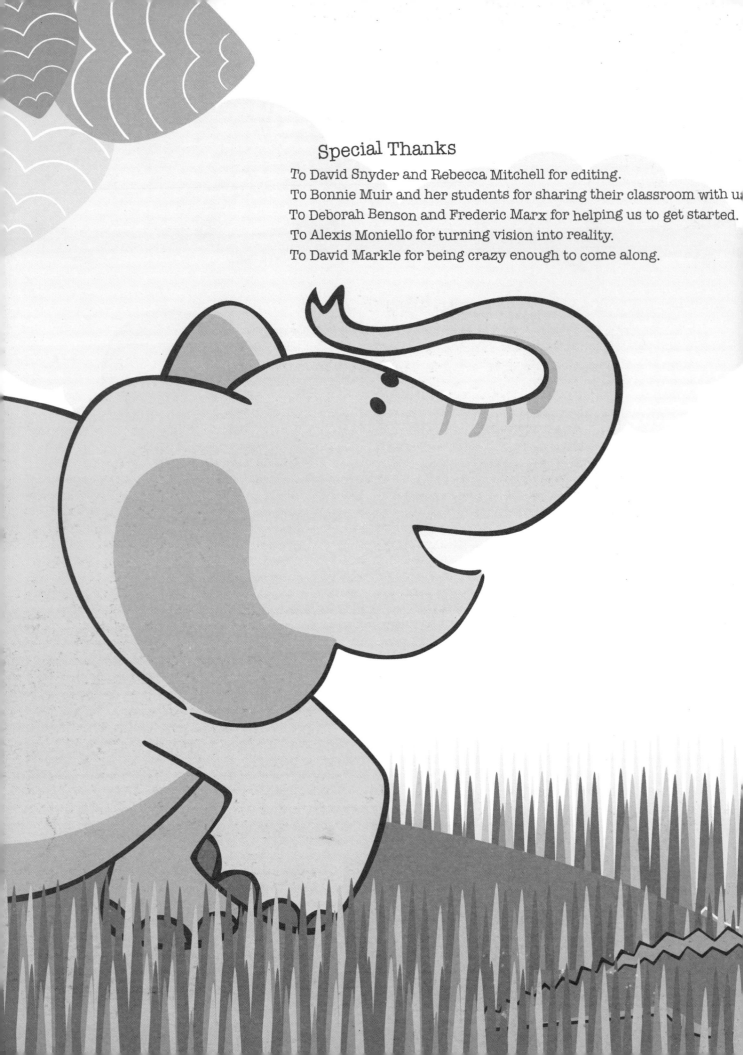

Special Thanks

To David Snyder and Rebecca Mitchell for editing.
To Bonnie Muir and her students for sharing their classroom with us.
To Deborah Benson and Frederic Marx for helping us to get started.
To Alexis Moniello for turning vision into reality.
To David Markle for being crazy enough to come along.